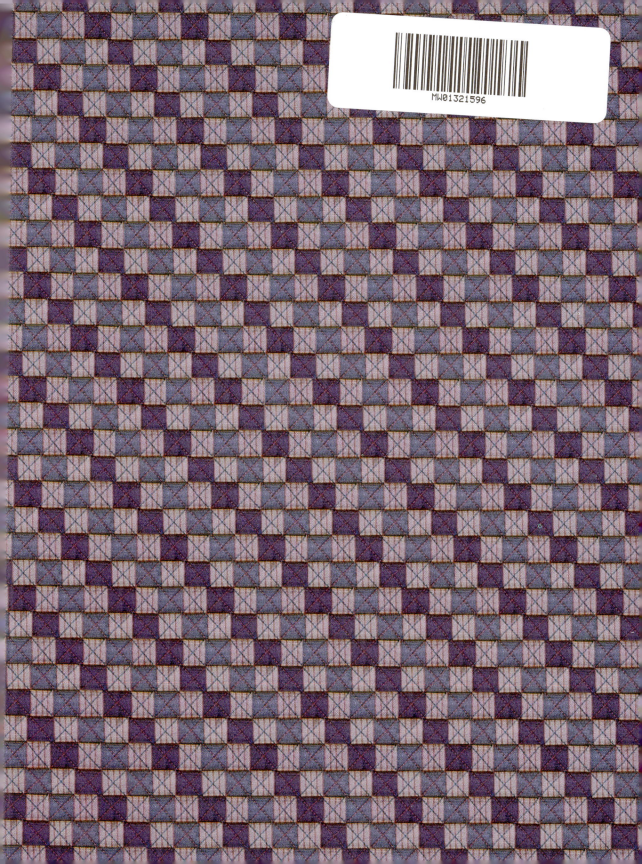

ISBN 0-921156-60-X

© 2000 Rubicon Publishing Inc.,
Oakville, Ontario, Canada

All rights reserved. Except for brief quotation for the purpose of review, no part of this publication may be reproduced, transmitted, or stored in any form or by any means without permission of the publisher.

Cover and *Title Page*
The Three Daughters of the Maharajah
Marion Spanjerdt
Wall panel in silks; 26" x 22"

WEAVING NEW RHYTHMS

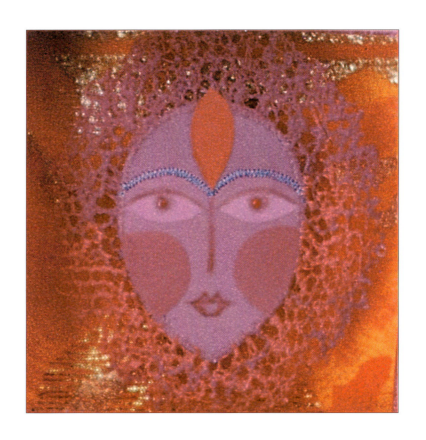

DIARY 2001

2001
WEAVING NEW RHYTHMS

So, tip toe as a dancer before music's start,

I see you eager to begin; and dance you must

Although new rhythms weave you unaware

From sunshine into shade...

Dorothy Livesay

Caribana (detail) D. Joyce Davies Quilt; 35 1/2" x 39"

There is a rhythm to nature, as there is to language. The rhythm varies from country to country and language to language. In nature we call these rhythms seasons, and in language they are poetry. In this diary marking the new millennium, we offer you a place to record the individual rhythms of your life, alongside the twining threads of our textile artists and the lyrical words of our poets.

Carol Milne-Smith *Editor*

Maxine Cowan *Designer*

Winter Birches **Sylvia Ridgway** Batik; size 26" x 40"

This **DIARY** belongs to

Name
_____

Address
_____
_____

City
_____

Province/State
_____

Country
_____

Postal/Zip code
_____

Work phone
_____

Home phone
_____

Email
_____

Emergency contact
_____
_____
_____
_____

2000

January
M	T	W	T	F	S	S
					1	2
3	4	5	6	7	8	9
10	11	12	13	14	15	16
17	18	19	20	21	22	23
24	25	26	27	28	29	30
31						

February
M	T	W	T	F	S	S
	1	2	3	4	5	6
7	8	9	10	11	12	13
14	15	16	17	18	19	20
21	22	23	24	25	26	27
28	29					

March
M	T	W	T	F	S	S
		1	2	3	4	5
6	7	8	9	10	11	12
13	14	15	16	17	18	19
20	21	22	23	24	25	26
27	28	29	30	31		

April
M	T	W	T	F	S	S
					1	2
3	4	5	6	7	8	9
10	11	12	13	14	15	16
17	18	19	20	21	22	23
24	25	26	27	28	29	30

May
M	T	W	T	F	S	S
1	2	3	4	5	6	7
8	9	10	11	12	13	14
15	16	17	18	19	20	21
22	23	24	25	26	27	28
29	30	31				

June
M	T	W	T	F	S	S
			1	2	3	4
5	6	7	8	9	10	11
12	13	14	15	16	17	18
19	20	21	22	23	24	25
26	27	28	29	30		

July
M	T	W	T	F	S	S
					1	2
3	4	5	6	7	8	9
10	11	12	13	14	15	16
17	18	19	20	21	22	23
24	25	26	27	28	29	30
31						

August
M	T	W	T	F	S	S
	1	2	3	4	5	6
7	8	9	10	11	12	13
14	15	16	17	18	19	20
21	22	23	24	25	26	27
28	29	30	31			

September
M	T	W	T	F	S	S
				1	2	3
4	5	6	7	8	9	10
11	12	13	14	15	16	17
18	19	20	21	22	23	24
25	26	27	28	29	30	

October
M	T	W	T	F	S	S
						1
2	3	4	5	6	7	8
9	10	11	12	13	14	15
16	17	18	19	20	21	22
23	24	25	26	27	28	29
30	31					

November
M	T	W	T	F	S	S
		1	2	3	4	5
6	7	8	9	10	11	12
13	14	15	16	17	18	19
20	21	22	23	24	25	26
27	28	29	30			

December
M	T	W	T	F	S	S
				1	2	3
4	5	6	7	8	9	10
11	12	13	14	15	16	17
18	19	20	21	22	23	24
25	26	27	28	29	30	31

2002

January
M	T	W	T	F	S	S
	1	2	3	4	5	6
7	8	9	10	11	12	13
14	15	16	17	18	19	20
21	22	23	24	25	26	27
28	29	30	31			

February
M	T	W	T	F	S	S
				1	2	3
4	5	6	7	8	9	10
11	12	13	14	15	16	17
18	19	20	21	22	23	24
25	26	27	28			

March
M	T	W	T	F	S	S
				1	2	3
4	5	6	7	8	9	10
11	12	13	14	15	16	17
18	19	20	21	22	23	24
25	26	27	28	29	30	31

April
M	T	W	T	F	S	S
1	2	3	4	5	6	7
8	9	10	11	12	13	14
15	16	17	18	19	20	21
22	23	24	25	26	27	28
29	30					

May
M	T	W	T	F	S	S
		1	2	3	4	5
6	7	8	9	10	11	12
13	14	15	16	17	18	19
20	21	22	23	24	25	26
27	28	29	30	31		

June
M	T	W	T	F	S	S
					1	2
3	4	5	6	7	8	9
10	11	12	13	14	15	16
17	18	19	20	21	22	23
24	25	26	27	28	29	30

July
M	T	W	T	F	S	S
1	2	3	4	5	6	7
8	9	10	11	12	13	14
15	16	17	18	19	20	21
22	23	24	25	26	27	28
29	30	31				

August
M	T	W	T	F	S	S
			1	2	3	4
5	6	7	8	9	10	11
12	13	14	15	16	17	18
19	20	21	22	23	24	25
26	27	28	29	30	31	

September
M	T	W	T	F	S	S
						1
2	3	4	5	6	7	8
9	10	11	12	13	14	15
16	17	18	19	20	21	22
23	24	25	26	27	28	29
30						

October
M	T	W	T	F	S	S
	1	2	3	4	5	6
7	8	9	10	11	12	13
14	15	16	17	18	19	20
21	22	23	24	25	26	27
28	29	30	31			

November
M	T	W	T	F	S	S
				1	2	3
4	5	6	7	8	9	10
11	12	13	14	15	16	17
18	19	20	21	22	23	24
25	26	27	28	29	30	

December
M	T	W	T	F	S	S
						1
2	3	4	5	6	7	8
9	10	11	12	13	14	15
16	17	18	19	20	21	22
23	24	25	26	27	28	29
30	31					

2001

JANUARY
M	T	W	T	F	S	S
1	2	3	4	5	6	7
8	9	10	11	12	13	14
15	16	17	18	19	20	21
22	23	24	25	26	27	28
29	30	31				

FEBRUARY
M	T	W	T	F	S	S
			1	2	3	4
5	6	7	8	9	10	11
12	13	14	15	16	17	18
19	20	21	22	23	24	25
26	27	28				

MARCH
M	T	W	T	F	S	S
			1	2	3	4
5	6	7	8	9	10	11
12	13	14	15	16	17	18
19	20	21	22	23	24	25
26	27	28	29	30	31	

APRIL
M	T	W	T	F	S	S
						1
2	3	4	5	6	7	8
9	10	11	12	13	14	15
16	17	18	19	20	21	22
23	24	25	26	27	28	29
30						

MAY
M	T	W	T	F	S	S
	1	2	3	4	5	6
7	8	9	10	11	12	13
14	15	16	17	18	19	20
21	22	23	24	25	26	27
28	29	30	31			

JUNE
M	T	W	T	F	S	S
				1	2	3
4	5	6	7	8	9	10
11	12	13	14	15	16	17
18	19	20	21	22	23	24
25	26	27	28	29	30	

JULY
M	T	W	T	F	S	S
						1
2	3	4	5	6	7	8
9	10	11	12	13	14	15
16	17	18	19	20	21	22
23	24	25	26	27	28	29
30	31					

AUGUST
M	T	W	T	F	S	S
		1	2	3	4	5
6	7	8	9	10	11	12
13	14	15	16	17	18	19
20	21	22	23	24	25	26
27	28	29	30	31		

SEPTEMBER
M	T	W	T	F	S	S
					1	2
3	4	5	6	7	8	9
10	11	12	13	14	15	16
17	18	19	20	21	22	23
24	25	26	27	28	29	30

OCTOBER
M	T	W	T	F	S	S
1	2	3	4	5	6	7
8	9	10	11	12	13	14
15	16	17	18	19	20	21
22	23	24	25	26	27	28
29	30	31				

NOVEMBER
M	T	W	T	F	S	S
			1	2	3	4
5	6	7	8	9	10	11
12	13	14	15	16	17	18
19	20	21	22	23	24	25
26	27	28	29	30		

DECEMBER
M	T	W	T	F	S	S
					1	2
3	4	5	6	7	8	9
10	11	12	13	14	15	16
17	18	19	20	21	22	23
24	25	26	27	28	29	30
31						

Holidays in 2001

January	1	New Year's Day
	15	Martin Luther King's Birthday
	24	Chinese New Year
February	14	Valentine's Day
	19	President's Day
March	17	St. Patrick's Day
	28	Ash Wednesday
April	8	Passover
	13	Good Friday
	15	Easter Sunday
	16	Palm Sunday
May	13	Mother's Day
	21	Victoria Day
	28	Memorial Day
June	17	Father's Day
	24	St. Jean Baptiste Day
July	1	Canada Day
	4	Independence Day, USA
August	6	Civic Holiday
September	3	Labour Day
	18	Rosh Hashanah
	27	Yom Kippur
October	8	Thanksgiving Day, Canada
	8	Columbus Day
	31	Halloween
November	11	Remembrance Day
	22	Thanksgiving Day, USA
December	10	Hanukah
	25	Christmas Day
	26	Boxing Day

Globos-Acapulco **William Hodge** Fabric Collage, bead embroidery; 31 1/2" x 25"

Birthdays and anniversaries

	date	name	occasion
January			
February			
March			
April			
May			
June			
July			
August			
September			

	date	name	occasion
October			
November			
December			

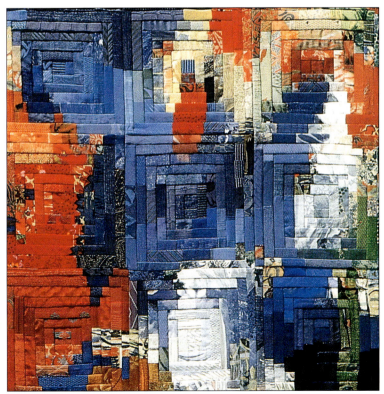

Blue Note **Marie-José Danzon** Quilt; 24" x 24"

I Know What's Beyond the Gate **Alma Newton** Fabric collage: 5'6" x 3'

JANUARY

This is the solstice, the still point

Of the sun, its cusp and midnight,

The year's threshold and unlocking, where the past

lets go of and becomes the future...

Margaret Atwood

JANUARY

Draw up a design for a quilt,
Begin a new way of creating,
Welcome the images of difference,
Seek ways to rebuild it
And make great
The pieces of fabric.

Elizabeth Ann Anderson

1 Monday

8
9
10
11
12
1
2
3
4
5
6

evening

special events

2 Tuesday

8
9
10
11
12
1
2
3
4
5
6

evening

special events

3 Wednesday

8
9
10
11
12
1
2
3
4
5
6

evening

special events

JANUARY

4 Thursday

8
9
10
11
12
1
2
3
4
5
6

evening

special events

5 Friday

8
9
10
11
12
1
2
3
4
5
6

evening

special events

6 Saturday

8
9
10
11
12
1
2
3
4
5

7 Sunday

January	M	T	W	T	F	S	S
	1	2	3	4	5	6	7
	8	9	10	11	12	13	14
	15	16	17	18	19	20	21
	22	23	24	25	26	27	28
	29	30	31				

JANUARY

*The crunching snowshoes and the stinging air,
And silence, frost and beauty everywhere.*

Archibald Lampman

8 Monday

8
9
10
11
12
1
2
3
4
5
6

evening

special events

9 Tuesday

8
9
10
11
12
1
2
3
4
5
6

evening

special events

10 Wednesday

8
9
10
11
12
1
2
3
4
5
6

evening

special events

J A N U A R Y

11 Thursday

8
9
10
11
12
1
2
3
4
5
6

evening

special events

12 Friday

8
9
10
11
12
1
2
3
4
5
6

evening

special events

13 Saturday

8
9
10
11
12
1
2
3
4
5

14 Sunday

January	M	T	W	T	F	S	S
	1	2	3	4	5	6	7
	8	9	10	11	12	13	14
	15	16	17	18	19	20	21
	22	23	24	25	26	27	28
	29	30	31				

JANUARY

Work is...the alarm clock going off on winter mornings when it's dark and cold...

Carol Shields

15 Monday

8
9
10
11
12
1
2
3
4
5
6

evening

special events

16 Tuesday

8
9
10
11
12
1
2
3
4
5
6

evening

special events

17 Wednesday

8
9
10
11
12
1
2
3
4
5
6

evening

special events

JANUARY

18 Thursday

8
9
10
11
12
1
2
3
4
5
6

evening

special events

19 Friday

8
9
10
11
12
1
2
3
4
5
6

evening

special events

20 Saturday

8
9
10
11
12
1
2
3
4
5

21 Sunday

January	M	T	W	T	F	S	S
	1	2	3	4	5	6	7
	8	9	10	11	12	13	14
	15	16	17	18	19	20	21
	22	23	24	25	26	27	28
	29	30	31				

JANUARY

That night I felt the winter in my veins
A joyous tremor of the icy glow...

W. Wilfred Campbell

22 Monday

8
9
10
11
12
1
2
3
4
5
6

evening

special events

23 Tuesday

8
9
10
11
12
1
2
3
4
5
6

evening

special events

24 Wednesday

8
9
10
11
12
1
2
3
4
5
6

evening

special events

JANUARY

25 **Thursday**

8
9
10
11
12
1
2
3
4
5
6

evening

special events

26 **Friday**

8
9
10
11
12
1
2
3
4
5
6

evening

special events

27 **Saturday**

8
9
10
11
12
1
2
3
4
5

28 **Sunday**

January	M	T	W	T	F	S	S
		1	2	3	4	5	6	7
	8	9	10	11	12	13	14
	15	16	17	18	19	20	21
	22	23	24	25	26	27	28
	29	30	31				

JANUARY

Winter, Time to eat fat
And watch hockey...

Margaret Atwood

29 **Monday**

8
9
10
11
12
1
2
3
4
5
6

evening

special events

30 **Tuesday**

8
9
10
11
12
1
2
3
4
5
6

evening

special events

31 **Wednesday**

8
9
10
11
12
1
2
3
4
5
6

evening

special events

F E B R U A R Y

1 **Thursday**

8
9
10
11
12
1
2
3
4
5
6

evening

special events

2 **Friday**

8
9
10
11
12
1
2
3
4
5
6

evening

special events

3 **Saturday**

8
9
10
11
12
1
2
3
4
5

4 **Sunday**

February	M	T	W	T	F	S	S
				1	2	3	4
	5	6	7	8	9	10	11
	12	13	14	15	16	17	18
	19	20	21	22	23	24	25
	26	27	28				

My Life Before The NHL **Deanne Fitzpatrick** Recycled wool cloth on burlap; 6' x 3'

FEBRUARY

My country's not a country, it's winter...
My garden's not a garden, it's the plains,
My road's not a road, it's the snow,
My country's not a country, it's winter.

Gilles Vigneault

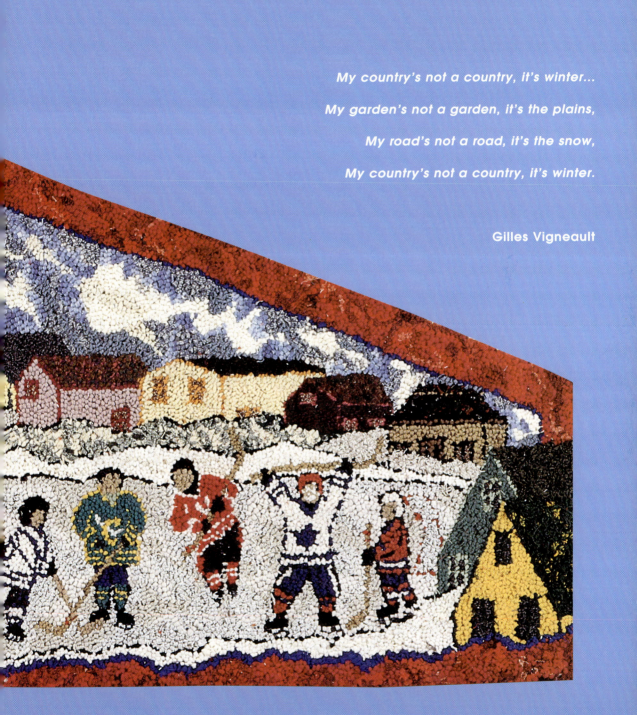

FEBRUARY

Soft fall the February snows, and hushed
Seems life's loud action, all its strife removed...

W. Wilfred Campbell

5 **Monday**

8
9
10
11
12
1
2
3
4
5
6

evening

special events

6 **Tuesday**

8
9
10
11
12
1
2
3
4
5
6

evening

special events

7 **Wednesday**

8
9
10
11
12
1
2
3
4
5
6

evening

special events

F E B R U A R Y

8 Thursday

8
9
10
11
12
1
2
3
4
5
6

evening

special events

9 Friday

8
9
10
11
12
1
2
3
4
5
6

evening

special events

10 Saturday

8
9
10
11
12
1
2
3
4
5

11 Sunday

February	M	T	W	T	F	S	S
				1	2	3	4
	5	6	7	8	9	10	11
	12	13	14	15	16	17	18
	19	20	21	22	23	24	25
	26	27	28				

FEBRUARY

Then kiss me!
Break your body into 1000 elements
Of energy,
Splash me with joy...

Dorothy Livesay

12 Monday

8
9
10
11
12
1
2
3
4
5
6

evening

special events

13 Tuesday

8
9
10
11
12
1
2
3
4
5
6

evening

special events

14 Wednesday

8
9
10
11
12
1
2
3
4
5
6

evening

special events

F E B R U A R Y

15 Thursday

8
9
10
11
12
1
2
3
4
5
6

evening

special events

16 Friday

8
9
10
11
12
1
2
3
4
5
6

evening

special events

17 Saturday

8
9
10
11
12
1
2
3
4
5

18 Sunday

February	M	T	W	T	F	S	S
				1	2	3	4
	5	6	7	8	9	10	11
	12	13	14	15	16	17	18
	19	20	21	22	23	24	25
	26	27	28				

FEBRUARY

Then she knew we women
Would keep the tribe alive...

Bad winters are women winters

Lenny Everson

19 Monday

- 8
- 9
- 10
- 11
- 12
- 1
- 2
- 3
- 4
- 5
- 6

evening

special events

20 Tuesday

- 8
- 9
- 10
- 11
- 12
- 1
- 2
- 3
- 4
- 5
- 6

evening

special events

21 Wednesday

- 8
- 9
- 10
- 11
- 12
- 1
- 2
- 3
- 4
- 5
- 6

evening

special events

FEBRUARY

22 Thursday

8
9
10
11
12
1
2
3
4
5
6

evening

special events

23 Friday

8
9
10
11
12
1
2
3
4
5
6

evening

special events

24 Saturday

8
9
10
11
12
1
2
3
4
5

25 Sunday

February	M	T	W	T	F	S	S
				1	2	3	4
	5	6	7	8	9	10	11
	12	13	14	15	16	17	18
	19	20	21	22	23	24	25
	26	27	28				

FEBRUARY

*I believe in fate, no alternative.
All the reasons we are who we are.*

Rita Joe

26 Monday

8
9
10
11
12
1
2
3
4
5
6

evening

special events

27 Tuesday

8
9
10
11
12
1
2
3
4
5
6

evening

special events

28 Wednesday

8
9
10
11
12
1
2
3
4
5
6

evening

special events

M A R C H

1 Thursday

8
9
10
11
12
1
2
3
4
5
6

evening

special events

2 Friday

8
9
10
11
12
1
2
3
4
5
6

evening

special events

3 Saturday

8
9
10
11
12
1
2
3
4
5

4 Sunday

March	M	T	W	T	F	S	S
				1	2	3	4
	5	6	7	8	9	10	11
	12	13	14	15	16	17	18
	19	20	21	22	23	24	25
	26	27	28	29	30	31	

Prayer Flags Jean L. Kares Hand-printed on cotton gauze; 32" x 40" each

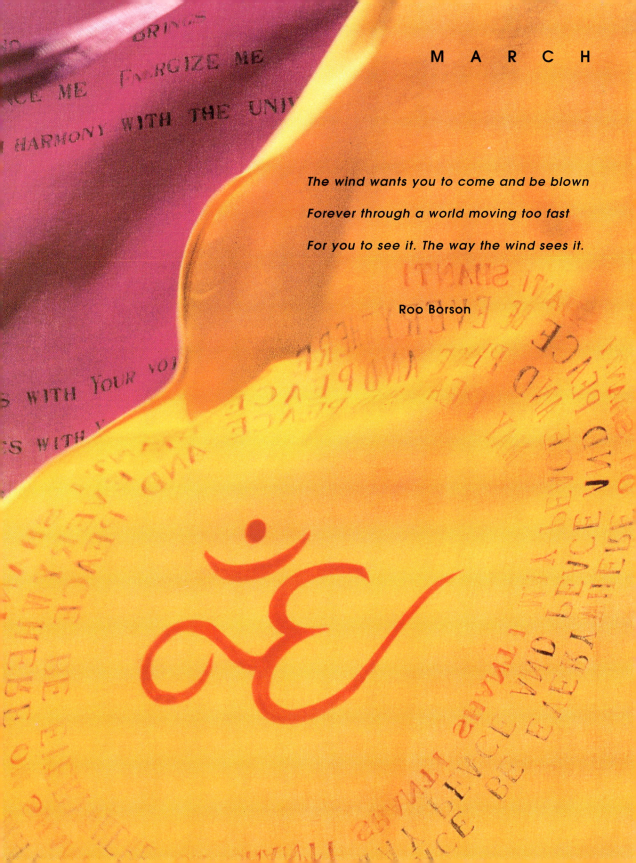

MARCH

The wind wants you to come and be blown

Forever through a world moving too fast

For you to see it. The way the wind sees it.

Roo Borson

MARCH

Happiness grows at our own fireside and is not to be picked in strangers' gardens.

Carol Shields

5 Monday

8
9
10
11
12
1
2
3
4
5
6

evening

special events

6 Tuesday

8
9
10
11
12
1
2
3
4
5
6

evening

special events

7 Wednesday

8
9
10
11
12
1
2
3
4
5
6

evening

special events

M A R C H

8 Thursday

8
9
10
11
12
1
2
3
4
5
6

evening

special events

9 Friday

8
9
10
11
12
1
2
3
4
5
6

evening

special events

10 Saturday

8
9
10
11
12
1
2
3
4
5

11 Sunday

March	M	T	W	T	F	S	S
				1	2	3	4
	5	6	7	8	9	10	11
	12	13	14	15	16	17	18
	19	20	21	22	23	24	25
	26	27	28	29	30	31	

MARCH

A little soup for the stomach's sake.
No — the soul's —

Ralph Gustafson

12 Monday

8
9
10
11
12
1
2
3
4
5
6

evening

special events

13 Tuesday

8
9
10
11
12
1
2
3
4
5
6

evening

special events

14 Wednesday

8
9
10
11
12
1
2
3
4
5
6

evening

special events

MARCH

15 Thursday

8
9
10
11
12
1
2
3
4
5
6

evening

special events

16 Friday

8
9
10
11
12
1
2
3
4
5
6

evening

special events

17 Saturday

8
9
10
11
12
1
2
3
4
5

18 Sunday

March	M	T	W	T	F	S	S
				1	2	3	4
	5	6	7	8	9	10	11
	12	13	14	15	16	17	18
	19	20	21	22	23	24	25
	26	27	28	29	30	31	

MARCH

*There is no season when gratitude seems
more naturally to fill our hearts, than at early dawn —
it is the renewal to us of our existence,
we feel that we have been cared for and preserved...*

Catherine Parr Traill

19 Monday

8
9
10
11
12
1
2
3
4
5
6

evening

special events

20 Tuesday

8
9
10
11
12
1
2
3
4
5
6

evening

special events

21 Wednesday

8
9
10
11
12
1
2
3
4
5
6

evening

special events

M A R C H

22 Thursday

8
9
10
11
12
1
2
3
4
5
6

evening

special events

23 Friday

8
9
10
11
12
1
2
3
4
5
6

evening

special events

24 Saturday

8
9
10
11
12
1
2
3
4
5

25 Sunday

March	M	T	W	T	F	S	S
			1	2	3	4
5	6	7	8	9	10	11
12	13	14	15	16	17	18
19	20	21	22	23	24	25
26	27	28	29	30	31	

MARCH

life isn't so bad   don't worry
spring will get here   don't worry

Robert Kroetsch

26 Monday

8
9
10
11
12
1
2
3
4
5
6

evening

special events

27 Tuesday

8
9
10
11
12
1
2
3
4
5
6

evening

special events

28 Wednesday

8
9
10
11
12
1
2
3
4
5
6

evening

special events

A P R I L

29 Thursday

8
9
10
11
12
1
2
3
4
5
6

evening

special events

30 Friday

8
9
10
11
12
1
2
3
4
5
6

evening

special events

31 Saturday

8
9
10
11
12
1
2
3
4
5

1 Sunday

April	M	T	W	T	F	S	S
							1
	2	3	4	5	6	7	8
	9	10	11	12	13	14	15
	16	17	18	19	20	21	22
	23	24	25	26	27	28	29
	30						

Untitled (from the Brassieres series) **Angelika Werth** Quilt; 47" x 65"

A P R I L

I am the spirit astir...

I am the life that thrills

In branch and bloom...

Charles G. D. Roberts

APRIL

...snow on green branches—
April has come at last.
The earth is astonished,
Maddened, by chlorophyll.

George Elliot Clarke

2 Monday

8
9
10
11
12
1
2
3
4
5
6

evening

special events

3 Tuesday

8
9
10
11
12
1
2
3
4
5
6

evening

special events

4 Wednesday

8
9
10
11
12
1
2
3
4
5
6

evening

special events

A P R I L

5 **Thursday**

8
9
10
11
12
1
2
3
4
5
6

evening

special events

6 **Friday**

8
9
10
11
12
1
2
3
4
5
6

evening

special events

7 **Saturday**

8
9
10
11
12
1
2
3
4
5

8 **Sunday**

April	M	T	W	T	F	S	S
							1
	2	3	4	5	6	7	8
	9	10	11	12	13	14	15
	16	17	18	19	20	21	22
	23	24	25	26	27	28	29
	30						

A P R I L

Church bells ring joyfully
Echoing soft and clear
All nature joins in sweet refrain
As Easter Morn is here

Laura Barbara Dixon

9 Monday

8
9
10
11
12
1
2
3
4
5
6

evening

special events

10 Tuesday

8
9
10
11
12
1
2
3
4
5
6

evening

special events

11 Wednesday

8
9
10
11
12
1
2
3
4
5
6

evening

special events

APRIL

12 Thursday

8
9
10
11
12
1
2
3
4
5
6

evening

special events

13 Friday

8
9
10
11
12
1
2
3
4
5
6

evening

special events

14 Saturday

8
9
10
11
12
1
2
3
4
5

15 Sunday

April	M	T	W	T	F	S	S
							1
	2	3	4	5	6	7	8
	9	10	11	12	13	14	15
	16	17	18	19	20	21	22
	23	24	25	26	27	28	29
	30						

APRIL

...the forsythia bush studs with flowers the golden tiara of April...

Miriam Waddington

16 Monday

8
9
10
11
12
1
2
3
4
5
6

evening

special events

17 Tuesday

8
9
10
11
12
1
2
3
4
5
6

evening

special events

18 Wednesday

8
9
10
11
12
1
2
3
4
5
6

evening

special events

A P R I L

19 Thursday

8
9
10
11
12
1
2
3
4
5
6

evening

special events

20 Friday

8
9
10
11
12
1
2
3
4
5
6

evening

special events

21 Saturday

8
9
10
11
12
1
2
3
4
5

22 Sunday

April	M	T	W	T	F	S	S
							1
	2	3	4	5	6	7	8
	9	10	11	12	13	14	15
	16	17	18	19	20	21	22
	23	24	25	26	27	28	29
	30						

APRIL

*One
red
cardinal
first shooting
flame
of
spring*

Raymond Souster

23 Monday | 24 Tuesday | 25 Wednesday

23 Monday	24 Tuesday	25 Wednesday
8	8	8
9	9	9
10	10	10
11	11	11
12	12	12
1	1	1
2	2	2
3	3	3
4	4	4
5	5	5
6	6	6
evening	evening	evening
special events	special events	special events

APRIL

26 **Thursday**

8
9
10
11
12
1
2
3
4
5
6

evening

special events

27 **Friday**

8
9
10
11
12
1
2
3
4
5
6

evening

special events

28 **Saturday**

8
9
10
11
12
1
2
3
4
5

29 **Sunday**

April	M	T	W	T	F	S	S
							1
	2	3	4	5	6	7	8
	9	10	11	12	13	14	15
	16	17	18	19	20	21	22
	23	24	25	26	27	28	29
	30						

Out of the black soil come pale flowers

A P R I L

David Helwig

30 Monday

8
9
10
11
12
1
2
3
4
5
6

evening

special events

1 Tuesday

8
9
10
11
12
1
2
3
4
5
6

evening

special events

2 Wednesday

8
9
10
11
12
1
2
3
4
5
6

evening

special events

M A Y

3 Thursday

8
9
10
11
12
1
2
3
4
5
6

evening

special events

4 Friday

8
9
10
11
12
1
2
3
4
5
6

evening

special events

5 Saturday

8
9
10
11
12
1
2
3
4
5

6 Sunday

May	M	T	W	T	F	S	S
		1	2	3	4	5	6
	7	8	9	10	11	12	13
	14	15	16	17	18	19	20
	21	22	23	24	25	26	27
	28	29	30	31			

May was a wonderful country;

All the world's children were in pilgrimage

To greet the summer...

                Miriam Waddington

MAY

I think I can (Detail: "Window onto Childhood") **Jane Coryell** Hand embroidery with button; 36" x 29"

MAY

My children...
I love them each day
As for the first time.

Marie-Claire Blais

7 Monday

8
9
10
11
12
1
2
3
4
5
6

evening

special events

8 Tuesday

8
9
10
11
12
1
2
3
4
5
6

evening

special events

9 Wednesday

8
9
10
11
12
1
2
3
4
5
6

evening

special events

M A Y

10 Thursday

8
9
10
11
12
1
2
3
4
5
6

evening

special events

11 Friday

8
9
10
11
12
1
2
3
4
5
6

evening

special events

12 Saturday

8
9
10
11
12
1
2
3
4
5

13 Sunday

May M T W T F S S
           1 2 3 4 5 6
      7 8 9 10 11 12 13
    14 15 16 17 18 19 20
    21 22 23 24 25 26 27
    28 29 30 31

M A Y

I quilt, planting sunflower patches in a pleasance of thick cotton

George Elliot Clarke

14 Monday

8
9
10
11
12
1
2
3
4
5
6

evening

special events

15 Tuesday

8
9
10
11
12
1
2
3
4
5
6

evening

special events

16 Wednesday

8
9
10
11
12
1
2
3
4
5
6

evening

special events

M A Y

17 Thursday

8
9
10
11
12
1
2
3
4
5
6

evening

special events

18 Friday

8
9
10
11
12
1
2
3
4
5
6

evening

special events

19 Saturday

8
9
10
11
12
1
2
3
4
5

20 Sunday

May	M	T	W	T	F	S	S
		1	2	3	4	5	6
	7	8	9	10	11	12	13
	14	15	16	17	18	19	20
	21	22	23	24	25	26	27
	28	29	30	31			

M A Y

The shape of prayer is that—
...saying everything
and saying nothing at all.

Phyllis Webb

21 **Monday**

8
9
10
11
12
1
2
3
4
5
6

evening

special events

22 **Tuesday**

8
9
10
11
12
1
2
3
4
5
6

evening

special events

23 **Wednesday**

8
9
10
11
12
1
2
3
4
5
6

evening

special events

M A Y

24 Thursday

8
9
10
11
12
1
2
3
4
5
6

evening

special events

25 Friday

8
9
10
11
12
1
2
3
4
5
6

evening

special events

26 Saturday

8
9
10
11
12
1
2
3
4
5

27 Sunday

May	M	T	W	T	F	S	S
		1	2	3	4	5	6
	7	8	9	10	11	12	13
	14	15	16	17	18	19	20
	21	22	23	24	25	26	27
	28	29	30	31			

MAY

*Today the leaves of the oaks, maples, beeches,
run with the warm wind
as I play with the children
on the slides and swings.*

David Helwig

28 Monday

8
9
10
11
12
1
2
3
4
5
6

evening

special events

29 Tuesday

8
9
10
11
12
1
2
3
4
5
6

evening

special events

30 Wednesday

8
9
10
11
12
1
2
3
4
5
6

evening

special events

J U N E

31 **Thursday**

8
9
10
11
12
1
2
3
4
5
6

evening

special events

1 **Friday**

8
9
10
11
12
1
2
3
4
5
6

evening

special events

2 **Saturday**

8
9
10
11
12
1
2
3
4
5

3 **Sunday**

June	M	T	W	T	F	S	S
					1	2	3
	4	5	6	7	8	9	10
	11	12	13	14	15	16	17
	18	19	20	21	22	23	24
	25	26	27	28	29	30	

Emblem/Endearment (Detail: Memento Series) **Jane Kidd** Tapestry; 36" x 36"

JUNE

...buy roses, roses, roses

To mingle with the nuptial myrtle; look

I strip the polish'd thorns from the stems,

The nuptial rose should be a stingless flower...

Isabella Valancy Crawford

JUNE

*We wed words to things, people to feelings, speak of a
True wedding of the mind and heart...*

bp Nichol

4 **Monday**

8
9
10
11
12
1
2
3
4
5
6

evening

special events

5 **Tuesday**

8
9
10
11
12
1
2
3
4
5
6

evening

special events

6 **Wednesday**

8
9
10
11
12
1
2
3
4
5
6

evening

special events

J U N E

7 Thursday

8
9
10
11
12
1
2
3
4
5
6

evening

special events

8 Friday

8
9
10
11
12
1
2
3
4
5
6

evening

special events

9 Saturday

8
9
10
11
12
1
2
3
4
5

10 Sunday

June	M	T	W	T	F	S	S
					1	2	3
	4	5	6	7	8	9	10
	11	12	13	14	15	16	17
	18	19	20	21	22	23	24
	25	26	27	28	29	30	

J U N E

During the day I laugh and during the night I sleep.

Leonard Cohen

11 Monday

8
9
10
11
12
1
2
3
4
5
6

evening

special events

12 Tuesday

8
9
10
11
12
1
2
3
4
5
6

evening

special events

13 Wednesday

8
9
10
11
12
1
2
3
4
5
6

evening

special events

J U N E

14 Thursday

8
9
10
11
12
1
2
3
4
5
6

evening

special events

15 Friday

8
9
10
11
12
1
2
3
4
5
6

evening

special events

16 Saturday

8
9
10
11
12
1
2
3
4
5

17 Sunday

June M T W T F S S
           1 2 3
      4 5 6 7 8 9 10
     11 12 13 14 15 16 17
     18 19 20 21 22 23 24
     25 26 27 28 29 30

JUNE

*The wheat was embroidering
All the spring morning,
Frail threads needled by sunshine like thin gold.*

Anne Marriott

18 Monday   19 Tuesday   20 Wednesday

18 Monday	19 Tuesday	20 Wednesday
8	8	8
9	9	9
10	10	10
11	11	11
12	12	12
1	1	1
2	2	2
3	3	3
4	4	4
5	5	5
6	6	6
evening	evening	evening
special events	special events	special events

JUNE

21 Thursday

8
9
10
11
12
1
2
3
4
5
6

evening

special events

22 Friday

8
9
10
11
12
1
2
3
4
5
6

evening

special events

23 Saturday

8
9
10
11
12
1
2
3
4
5

24 Sunday

June	M	T	W	T	F	S	S
					1	2	3
	4	5	6	7	8	9	10
	11	12	13	14	15	16	17
	18	19	20	21	22	23	24
	25	26	27	28	29	30	

JUNE

A country of quiescence and still distance
a lean land
not like the fat south...

Al Purdy

25 **Monday**	26 **Tuesday**	27 **Wednesday**
8	8	8
9	9	9
10	10	10
11	11	11
12	12	12
1	1	1
2	2	2
3	3	3
4	4	4
5	5	5
6	6	6
evening	evening	evening
special events	special events	special events

JULY

28 Thursday

8
9
10
11
12
1
2
3
4
5
6

evening

special events

29 Friday

8
9
10
11
12
1
2
3
4
5
6

evening

special events

30 Saturday

8
9
10
11
12
1
2
3
4
5

1 Sunday

July	M	T	W	T	F	S	S
							1
	2	3	4	5	6	7	8
	9	10	11	12	13	14	15
	16	17	18	19	20	21	22
	23	24	25	26	27	28	29
	30	31					

Field Notes (detail) **Dorothy Caldwell** Indigo dyeing, quilt; size unknown

JULY

Taste a thesis on your tongue,

Honey, lemon, spring sprung water

loaded with geology.

Skin and flush of peaches, red

Tomatoes picked and bitten in the sun

All gush the juice and seed of summer

To the learned mouth.

                Anne Wilkinson

JULY

*Bees are truck drivers of the sky
who burrow into diners of flowers
to be fed therein, or overhauled.*

Joe Rosenblatt

2 Monday

8
9
10
11
12
1
2
3
4
5
6

evening

special events

3 Tuesday

8
9
10
11
12
1
2
3
4
5
6

evening

special events

4 Wednesday

8
9
10
11
12
1
2
3
4
5
6

evening

special events

J U L Y

5 **Thursday**

8
9
10
11
12
1
2
3
4
5
6

evening

special events

6 **Friday**

8
9
10
11
12
1
2
3
4
5
6

evening

special events

7 **Saturday**

8
9
10
11
12
1
2
3
4
5

8 **Sunday**

July	M	T	W	T	F	S	S
							1
	2	3	4	5	6	7	8
	9	10	11	12	13	14	15
	16	17	18	19	20	21	22
	23	24	25	26	27	28	29
	30	31					

JULY

*Life for my kid
Is a hammock swinging...*

Dorothy Livesay

9 Monday

8
9
10
11
12
1
2
3
4
5
6

evening

special events

10 Tuesday

8
9
10
11
12
1
2
3
4
5
6

evening

special events

11 Wednesday

8
9
10
11
12
1
2
3
4
5
6

evening

special events

J U L Y

12 **Thursday**

8
9
10
11
12
1
2
3
4
5
6

evening

special events

13 **Friday**

8
9
10
11
12
1
2
3
4
5
6

evening

special events

14 **Saturday**

8
9
10
11
12
1
2
3
4
5

15 **Sunday**

July	M	T	W	T	F	S	S
							1
	2	3	4	5	6	7	8
	9	10	11	12	13	14	15
	16	17	18	19	20	21	22
	23	24	25	26	27	28	29
	30	31					

JULY

*She may yearn to know the true state of the garden,
But she wants even more to be part of its mysteries...*

Carol Shields

16 Monday

8
9
10
11
12
1
2
3
4
5
6

evening

special events

17 Tuesday

8
9
10
11
12
1
2
3
4
5
6

evening

special events

18 Wednesday

8
9
10
11
12
1
2
3
4
5
6

evening

special events

JULY

19 Thursday

8
9
10
11
12
1
2
3
4
5
6

evening

special events

20 Friday

8
9
10
11
12
1
2
3
4
5
6

evening

special events

21 Saturday

8
9
10
11
12
1
2
3
4
5

22 Sunday

July M T W T F S S
                  1
      2 3 4 5 6 7 8
      9 10 11 12 13 14 15
     16 17 18 19 20 21 22
     23 24 25 26 27 28 29
     30 31

JULY

*The mollusk...tells the ocean's tale
to ears of children listening...*

Raymond Queneau

23 Monday

8
9
10
11
12
1
2
3
4
5
6

evening

special events

24 Tuesday

8
9
10
11
12
1
2
3
4
5
6

evening

special events

25 Wednesday

8
9
10
11
12
1
2
3
4
5
6

evening

special events

JULY

26 Thursday

8
9
10
11
12
1
2
3
4
5
6

evening

special events

27 Friday

8
9
10
11
12
1
2
3
4
5
6

evening

special events

28 Saturday

8
9
10
11
12
1
2
3
4
5

29 Sunday

July	M	T	W	T	F	S	S
							1
	2	3	4	5	6	7	8
	9	10	11	12	13	14	15
	16	17	18	19	20	21	22
	23	24	25	26	27	28	29
	30	31					

JULY

It is like a treacle, the world.
I am caught in its golden threads,
a fly in a honey pot.

P. K. Page

30 Monday

8
9
10
11
12
1
2
3
4
5
6

evening

special events

31 Tuesday

8
9
10
11
12
1
2
3
4
5
6

evening

special events

1 Wednesday

8
9
10
11
12
1
2
3
4
5
6

evening

special events

AUGUST

2 Thursday

8
9
10
11
12
1
2
3
4
5
6

evening

special events

3 Friday

8
9
10
11
12
1
2
3
4
5
6

evening

special events

4 Saturday

8
9
10
11
12
1
2
3
4
5

5 Sunday

August	M	T	W	T	F	S	S
			1	2	3	4	5
	6	7	8	9	10	11	12
	13	14	15	16	17	18	19
	20	21	22	23	24	25	26
	27	28	29	30	31		

Dream Woman With Fish **Margi Hennen** Doll: approximately 15"

AUGUST

...a fistful of gathered

pebbles there was no point

in taking home, dropped on a beachful

of other coloured pebbles...

Margaret Atwood

AUGUST

August is laughing across the sky...

Pauline Johnson

6 Monday

8
9
10
11
12
1
2
3
4
5
6

evening

special events

7 Tuesday

8
9
10
11
12
1
2
3
4
5
6

evening

special events

8 Wednesday

8
9
10
11
12
1
2
3
4
5
6

evening

special events

A U G U S T

9 Thursday

8
9
10
11
12
1
2
3
4
5
6

evening

special events

10 Friday

8
9
10
11
12
1
2
3
4
5
6

evening

special events

11 Saturday

8
9
10
11
12
1
2
3
4
5

12 Sunday

August	M	T	W	T	F	S	S
			1	2	3	4	5
	6	7	8	9	10	11	12
	13	14	15	16	17	18	19
	20	21	22	23	24	25	26
	27	28	29	30	31		

AUGUST

the world, chuckling sideways
tossed me off
left me wildly treading air
to catch up.

Dorothy Livesay

13 Monday

8
9
10
11
12
1
2
3
4
5
6

evening

special events

14 Tuesday

8
9
10
11
12
1
2
3
4
5
6

evening

special events

15 Wednesday

8
9
10
11
12
1
2
3
4
5
6

evening

special events

A U G U S T

16 Thursday

8
9
10
11
12
1
2
3
4
5
6

evening

special events

17 Friday

8
9
10
11
12
1
2
3
4
5
6

evening

special events

18 Saturday

8
9
10
11
12
1
2
3
4
5

19 Sunday

August	M	T	W	T	F	S	S
			1	2	3	4	5
	6	7	8	9	10	11	12
	13	14	15	16	17	18	19
	20	21	22	23	24	25	26
	27	28	29	30	31		

AUGUST

*This day she picked the roses absently,
and shook the fairy petals into her little sweet grass basket
with the air of a woman whose thoughts were far away.*

Lucy Maud Montgomery

20 Monday

8
9
10
11
12
1
2
3
4
5
6

evening

special events

21 Tuesday

8
9
10
11
12
1
2
3
4
5
6

evening

special events

22 Wednesday

8
9
10
11
12
1
2
3
4
5
6

evening

special events

AUGUST

23 Thursday

8
9
10
11
12
1
2
3
4
5
6

evening

special events

24 Friday

8
9
10
11
12
1
2
3
4
5
6

evening

special events

25 Saturday

8
9
10
11
12
1
2
3
4
5

26 Sunday

August	M	T	W	T	F	S	S
			1	2	3	4	5
	6	7	8	9	10	11	12
	13	14	15	16	17	18	19
	20	21	22	23	24	25	26
	27	28	29	30	31		

AUGUST

Poetry, rocks, and husbands—
all these can be found on a beach...

G. E. Morgan

27 Monday

8
9
10
11
12
1
2
3
4
5
6

evening

special events

28 Tuesday

8
9
10
11
12
1
2
3
4
5
6

evening

special events

29 Wednesday

8
9
10
11
12
1
2
3
4
5
6

evening

special events

SEPTEMBER

30 Thursday

8
9
10
11
12
1
2
3
4
5
6

evening

special events

31 Friday

8
9
10
11
12
1
2
3
4
5
6

evening

special events

1 Saturday

8
9
10
11
12
1
2
3
4
5

2 Sunday

September	M	T	W	T	F	S	S
						1	2
	3	4	5	6	7	8	9
	10	11	12	13	14	15	16
	17	18	19	20	21	22	23
	24	25	26	27	28	29	30

SEPTEMBER

Muffle the wind;

Silence the clock;

Muzzle the mice

Curb the small talk;

Cure the hinge-squeak;

Banish the thunder.

Let me sit silent

Let me wonder

A. M. Klein

SEPTEMBER

Work's not just sitting in the corners of shadowy libraries and producing beautiful little monographs...
It's the alarm clock going off...

Carol Shields

3 Monday

8
9
10
11
12
1
2
3
4
5
6

evening

special events

4 Tuesday

8
9
10
11
12
1
2
3
4
5
6

evening

special events

5 Wednesday

8
9
10
11
12
1
2
3
4
5
6

evening

special events

S E P T E M B E R

6 Thursday

8
9
10
11
12
1
2
3
4
5
6

evening

special events

7 Friday

8
9
10
11
12
1
2
3
4
5
6

evening

special events

8 Saturday

8
9
10
11
12
1
2
3
4
5

9 Sunday

September	M	T	W	T	F	S	S
						1	2
	3	4	5	6	7	8	9
	10	11	12	13	14	15	16
	17	18	19	20	21	22	23
	24	25	26	27	28	29	30

SEPTEMBER

The best teacher lodges an intent not in the mind but in the heart.

Anne Michaels

10 Monday

8
9
10
11
12
1
2
3
4
5
6

evening

special events

11 Tuesday

8
9
10
11
12
1
2
3
4
5
6

evening

special events

12 Wednesday

8
9
10
11
12
1
2
3
4
5
6

evening

special events

SEPTEMBER

13 Thursday

8
9
10
11
12
1
2
3
4
5
6

evening

special events

14 Friday

8
9
10
11
12
1
2
3
4
5
6

evening

special events

15 Saturday

8
9
10
11
12
1
2
3
4
5

16 Sunday

September	M	T	W	T	F	S	S
						1	2
	3	4	5	6	7	8	9
	10	11	12	13	14	15	16
	17	18	19	20	21	22	23
	24	25	26	27	28	29	30

SEPTEMBER

*Women are breadwinners perforce
When their pay is their sole resource,
Or when couples aspire to arrive
At a house — not a cell in a hive*

Margaret Avison

17 Monday

8
9
10
11
12
1
2
3
4
5
6

evening

special events

18 Tuesday

8
9
10
11
12
1
2
3
4
5
6

evening

special events

19 Wednesday

8
9
10
11
12
1
2
3
4
5
6

evening

special events

SEPTEMBER

20 Thursday

8
9
10
11
12
1
2
3
4
5
6

evening

special events

21 Friday

8
9
10
11
12
1
2
3
4
5
6

evening

special events

22 Saturday

8
9
10
11
12
1
2
3
4
5

23 Sunday

September	M	T	W	T	F	S	S
						1	2
	3	4	5	6	7	8	9
	10	11	12	13	14	15	16
	17	18	19	20	21	22	23
	24	25	26	27	28	29	30

SEPTEMBER

*The picnic chairs
piled by the summer pavilion
towered like a paper dragon.*

David Helwig

24 Monday

8
9
10
11
12
1
2
3
4
5
6

evening

special events

25 Tuesday

8
9
10
11
12
1
2
3
4
5
6

evening

special events

26 Wednesday

8
9
10
11
12
1
2
3
4
5
6

evening

special events

S E P T E M B E R

27 Thursday

8
9
10
11
12
1
2
3
4
5
6

evening

special events

28 Friday

8
9
10
11
12
1
2
3
4
5
6

evening

special events

29 Saturday

8
9
10
11
12
1
2
3
4
5

30 Sunday

September	M	T	W	T	F	S	S
						1	2
	3	4	5	6	7	8	9
	10	11	12	13	14	15	16
	17	18	19	20	21	22	23
	24	25	26	27	28	29	30

Prairie Vista 1995 **Myrna Harris** Dyed and felted wool landscape; size 44" x 24"

OCTOBER

Now by the brook the maple leans

With all its glory spread,

And all the sumachs on the hills

Have turned their green to red

W. Wilfred Campbell

OCTOBER

In her cupboard
A pair of shoes sat on their haunches,
Crinkling up their toes
In dumb expectancy...

Dorothy Livesay

1 Monday

8
9
10
11
12
1
2
3
4
5
6

evening

special events

2 Tuesday

8
9
10
11
12
1
2
3
4
5
6

evening

special events

3 Wednesday

8
9
10
11
12
1
2
3
4
5
6

evening

special events

OCTOBER

4 Thursday

8
9
10
11
12
1
2
3
4
5
6

evening

special events

5 Friday

8
9
10
11
12
1
2
3
4
5
6

evening

special events

6 Saturday

8
9
10
11
12
1
2
3
4
5

7 Sunday

October	M	T	W	T	F	S	S
		1	2	3	4	5	6	7
	8	9	10	11	12	13	14
	15	16	17	18	19	20	21
	22	23	24	25	26	27	28
	29	30	31				

OCTOBER

*Inside the pumpkin   I feel much better
I feel   loyalty to my pioneering
ancestors...*

Robert Kroetsch

8 Monday

8
9
10
11
12
1
2
3
4
5
6

evening

special events

9 Tuesday

8
9
10
11
12
1
2
3
4
5
6

evening

special events

10 Wednesday

8
9
10
11
12
1
2
3
4
5
6

evening

special events

OCTOBER

11 Thursday

8
9
10
11
12
1
2
3
4
5
6

evening

special events

12 Friday

8
9
10
11
12
1
2
3
4
5
6

evening

special events

13 Saturday

8
9
10
11
12
1
2
3
4
5

14 Sunday

October	M	T	W	T	F	S	S
	1	2	3	4	5	6	7
	8	9	10	11	12	13	14
	15	16	17	18	19	20	21
	22	23	24	25	26	27	28
	29	30	31				

OCTOBER

*There is a joy of being, which you
Must be still and learn.*

Dennis Lee

15 Monday

8
9
10
11
12
1
2
3
4
5
6

evening

special events

16 Tuesday

8
9
10
11
12
1
2
3
4
5
6

evening

special events

17 Wednesday

8
9
10
11
12
1
2
3
4
5
6

evening

special events

OCTOBER

18 Thursday

8
9
10
11
12
1
2
3
4
5
6

evening

special events

19 Friday

8
9
10
11
12
1
2
3
4
5
6

evening

special events

20 Saturday

8
9
10
11
12
1
2
3
4
5

21 Sunday

October	M	T	W	T	F	S	S
	1	2	3	4	5	6	7
	8	9	10	11	12	13	14
	15	16	17	18	19	20	21
	22	23	24	25	26	27	28
	29	30	31				

OCTOBER

The lifelong day the elvish leaves
Danced with their shadows on the floor;
And the lost children of the wind
Went straying homeward by our door.

Bliss Carman

22 Monday

8
9
10
11
12
1
2
3
4
5
6

evening

special events

23 Tuesday

8
9
10
11
12
1
2
3
4
5
6

evening

special events

24 Wednesday

8
9
10
11
12
1
2
3
4
5
6

evening

special events

OCTOBER

25 Thursday

- 8
- 9
- 10
- 11
- 12
- 1
- 2
- 3
- 4
- 5
- 6

evening

special events

26 Friday

- 8
- 9
- 10
- 11
- 12
- 1
- 2
- 3
- 4
- 5
- 6

evening

special events

27 Saturday

- 8
- 9
- 10
- 11
- 12
- 1
- 2
- 3
- 4
- 5

28 Sunday

October	M	T	W	T	F	S	S
	1	2	3	4	5	6	7
	8	9	10	11	12	13	14
	15	16	17	18	19	20	21
	22	23	24	25	26	27	28
	29	30	31				

OCTOBER

I opened my eyes at the break of dawn
To see white frost on the Autumn lawn

Laura Barbara Dixon

29 Monday

8
9
10
11
12
1
2
3
4
5
6

evening

special events

30 Tuesday

8
9
10
11
12
1
2
3
4
5
6

evening

special events

31 Wednesday

8
9
10
11
12
1
2
3
4
5
6

evening

special events

NOVEMBER

1 Thursday

8
9
10
11
12
1
2
3
4
5
6

evening

special events

2 Friday

8
9
10
11
12
1
2
3
4
5
6

evening

special events

3 Saturday

8
9
10
11
12
1
2
3
4
5

4 Sunday

November	M	T	W	T	F	S	S
				1	2	3	4
	5	6	7	8	9	10	11
	12	13	14	15	16	17	18
	19	20	21	22	23	24	25
	26	27	28	29	30		

Garnished Pouch **Beverley McInnes** Appliquéd and beaded purse; 9 1/2" x 7"

But sometimes the world disrobes,

slips its dress off a shoulder,

stops time for a beat.

If we look up at that moment,

it's not due to any ability of ours

to pierce the darkness,

it's the world's brief bestowal.

Anne Michaels

NOVEMBER

...as I could not aid in subduing the enemies of my beloved country with my arm, I did what little I could to serve the good cause with my pen.

Susanna Moodie

5 Monday

8
9
10
11
12
1
2
3
4
5
6

evening

special events

6 Tuesday

8
9
10
11
12
1
2
3
4
5
6

evening

special events

7 Wednesday

8
9
10
11
12
1
2
3
4
5
6

evening

special events

N O V E M B E R

8 Thursday

8
9
10
11
12
1
2
3
4
5
6

evening

special events

9 Friday

8
9
10
11
12
1
2
3
4
5
6

evening

special events

10 Saturday

8
9
10
11
12
1
2
3
4
5

11 Sunday

November	M	T	W	T	F	S	S
				1	2	3	4
	5	6	7	8	9	10	11
	12	13	14	15	16	17	18
	19	20	21	22	23	24	25
	26	27	28	29	30		

NOVEMBER

On a solitary rock they stood
and counted the stitches
in the night sky.

G. E. Morgan

12 Monday

8
9
10
11
12
1
2
3
4
5
6

evening

special events

13 Tuesday

8
9
10
11
12
1
2
3
4
5
6

evening

special events

14 Wednesday

8
9
10
11
12
1
2
3
4
5
6

evening

special events

N O V E M B E R

15 Thursday

8
9
10
11
12
1
2
3
4
5
6

evening

special events

16 Friday

8
9
10
11
12
1
2
3
4
5
6

evening

special events

17 Saturday

8
9
10
11
12
1
2
3
4
5

18 Sunday

November M T W T F S S
               1 2 3 4
5 6 7 8 9 10 11
12 13 14 15 16 17 18
19 20 21 22 23 24 25
26 27 28 29 30

NOVEMBER

*...I see
the importance of family,
they remember the same things.*

Sparling Mills

19 Monday

8
9
10
11
12
1
2
3
4
5
6

evening

special events

20 Tuesday

8
9
10
11
12
1
2
3
4
5
6

evening

special events

21 Wednesday

8
9
10
11
12
1
2
3
4
5
6

evening

special events

N O V E M B E R

22 Thursday

8
9
10
11
12
1
2
3
4
5
6

evening

special events

23 Friday

8
9
10
11
12
1
2
3
4
5
6

evening

special events

24 Saturday

8
9
10
11
12
1
2
3
4
5

25 Sunday

November	M	T	W	T	F	S	S
			1	2	3	4
5	6	7	8	9	10	11
12	13	14	15	16	17	18
19	20	21	22	23	24	25
26	27	28	29	30		

NOVEMBER

The hills grow wintery white, and bleak winds moan
About the naked uplands. I alone
Am neither sad, nor shelterless, nor grey,
Wrapped round with thought, content to watch and dream

Archibald Lampman

26 Monday

8
9
10
11
12
1
2
3
4
5
6

evening

special events

27 Tuesday

8
9
10
11
12
1
2
3
4
5
6

evening

special events

28 Wednesday

8
9
10
11
12
1
2
3
4
5
6

evening

special events

D E C E M B E R

29 Thursday

8
9
10
11
12
1
2
3
4
5
6

evening

special events

30 Friday

8
9
10
11
12
1
2
3
4
5
6

evening

special events

1 Saturday

8
9
10
11
12
1
2
3
4
5

2 Sunday

December	M	T	W	T	F	S	S
						1	2
	3	4	5	6	7	8	9
	10	11	12	13	14	15	16
	17	18	19	20	21	22	23
	24	25	26	27	28	29	30
	31						

I hug life gently, tenderly each day;

I wake to find I have it and it's mine,

Mine to enjoy and make of, what I can...

Linda M. Brissett

Embellished Box **Christel Wille** Beaded box; size 5" x 5"

DECEMBER

The Milkweed Angel (detail) **Sybil Rampen** Milkweed silk and seeds stitched between plastic film; 4" x 4"

DECEMBER

*There is no chill so deep that
cannot be warmed with a kiss.*

G. E. Morgan

3 **Monday**   4 **Tuesday**   5 **Wednesday**

8

9

10

11

12

1

2

3

4

5

6

evening

special events

D E C E M B E R

6 Thursday

8
9
10
11
12
1
2
3
4
5
6

evening

special events

7 Friday

8
9
10
11
12
1
2
3
4
5
6

evening

special events

8 Saturday

8
9
10
11
12
1
2
3
4
5

9 Sunday

December	M	T	W	T	F	S	S
						1	2
	3	4	5	6	7	8	9
	10	11	12	13	14	15	16
	17	18	19	20	21	22	23
	24	25	26	27	28	29	30
	31						

DECEMBER

When the zenith moon is round,
And snow-wraiths gather and run,
And there is set no bound
To love beneath the sun...

Bliss Carman

10 Monday

8
9
10
11
12
1
2
3
4
5
6

evening

special events

11 Tuesday

8
9
10
11
12
1
2
3
4
5
6

evening

special events

12 Wednesday

8
9
10
11
12
1
2
3
4
5
6

evening

special events

DECEMBER

13 Thursday

8
9
10
11
12
1
2
3
4
5
6

evening

special events

14 Friday

8
9
10
11
12
1
2
3
4
5
6

evening

special events

15 Saturday

8
9
10
11
12
1
2
3
4
5

16 Sunday

December	M	T	W	T	F	S	S
						1	2
	3	4	5	6	7	8	9
	10	11	12	13	14	15	16
	17	18	19	20	21	22	23
	24	25	26	27	28	29	30
	31						

DECEMBER

My old face a new face growing
Childlike and rounded
Unwrinkled, unbounded
Holidaying
At infinity's station!

Dorothy Livesay

17 Monday

8
9
10
11
12
1
2
3
4
5
6

evening

special events

18 Tuesday

8
9
10
11
12
1
2
3
4
5
6

evening

special events

19 Wednesday

8
9
10
11
12
1
2
3
4
5
6

evening

special events

DECEMBER

20 Thursday

8
9
10
11
12
1
2
3
4
5
6

evening

special events

21 Friday

8
9
10
11
12
1
2
3
4
5
6

evening

special events

22 Saturday

8
9
10
11
12
1
2
3
4
5

23 Sunday

December	M	T	W	T	F	S	S
						1	2
	3	4	5	6	7	8	9
	10	11	12	13	14	15	16
	17	18	19	20	21	22	23
	24	25	26	27	28	29	30
	31						

DECEMBER

*...the green wreaths
festive and prickly, with their red
holly berries...*

Margaret Atwood

24 Monday

8
9
10
11
12
1
2
3
4
5
6

evening

special events

25 Tuesday

8
9
10
11
12
1
2
3
4
5
6

evening

special events

26 Wednesday

8
9
10
11
12
1
2
3
4
5
6

evening

special events

DECEMBER

27 Thursday

8
9
10
11
12
1
2
3
4
5
6

evening

special events

28 Friday

8
9
10
11
12
1
2
3
4
5
6

evening

special events

29 Saturday

8
9
10
11
12
1
2
3
4
5

30 Sunday

December	M	T	W	T	F	S	S
						1	2
	3	4	5	6	7	8	9
	10	11	12	13	14	15	16
	17	18	19	20	21	22	23
	24	25	26	27	28	29	30
	31						

DECEMBER

*Don't you remember that long, last waltz...
that would blend like an angel-song in
the bliss of the coming year?*

Robert Service

31 Monday

8
9
10
11
12
1
2
3
4
5
6

evening

special events

1 Tuesday

8
9
10
11
12
1
2
3
4
5
6

evening

special events

2 Wednesday

8
9
10
11
12
1
2
3
4
5
6

evening

special events

JANUARY
2 0 0 2

3 Thursday

8
9
10
11
12
1
2
3
4
5
6

evening

special events

4 Friday

8
9
10
11
12
1
2
3
4
5
6

evening

special events

5 Saturday

8
9
10
11
12
1
2
3
4
5

6 Sunday

January	M	T	W	T	F	S	S
		1	2	3	4	5	6
	7	8	9	10	11	12	13
	14	15	16	17	18	19	20
	21	22	23	24	25	26	27
	28	29	30	31			

Spring Diva #1 **Susan Cain** Doll: 4' x 2'6"

NOTES

*We will go around
in these circles for a time,
winter summer winter...
This is a good thought.*
Margaret Atwood

Frequently used numbers

Name   Phone

Name   Phone

Lily of the West Travelling to the Light (detail) **Betty Weaver** Woven panel; size unknown

ARTISTS

Susan Cain was educated both in the United States and in Canada. Her work is mostly three-dimensional, incorporating a variety of materials - painted fabric, wood, wire, metal, and found objects. Her Diva Series arise from the seasonal equinoxes - a celebration of the cycles of the natural world.

Dorothy Caldwell One of Canada's premier textile artists, Caldwell won the Bronfman Award in 1990. She has executed major architectural commissions and her work is in many permanent collections including The Museum of Civilisation and the Canadian consulate in Bangkok, Thailand. Caldwell's work incorporates the North American quilting traditions with resist and discharged dyeing techniques. Landscape is often the starting point for her work. Japan is a major influence both as a source of indigo dyeing practices and a shared belief with other artists in the integration of historical work in modern contexts.

Rosalyn Cherry-Soleil Cherry-Soleil's early love for sewing and knitting took her into fashion - designing hand-loomed ladies' high-fashion knitted clothing under the label of Marnie Knits. In 1992, she began to explore and combine paint with collage and needlepoint. She has since added fabric appliqué and photo-transfer, among others, to her needlepoint. Her work is often autobiographical.

Jane Coryell is both an art education expert and a textile artist. Dr. Coryell has taught the integration of studio work with history and appreciation in high schools, universities, and at conferences. As a fabric artist, Coryell has created embroideries in juried exhibitions and worked extensively with the Oakville (Ontario) Stitchery Guild. As a set/costume designer for 32 productions in community theatre, she has earned four nominations and won four awards for Best Design.

Marie-José Danzon was born in France where she received her education, training, and work experience before moving to Toronto, Ontario. Over a 20-year period, Danzon's work in pieced-quilt fibre art has evolved from traditional geometric patterns in unusual colour harmonies to highly painterly compositions based on an extraordinary variety of fabrics. "I just listen to my fabrics," said Danzon. Her works (mostly commissioned) are in private collections in North America and Europe.

D. Joyce Davies was born in Winnipeg, Manitoba and currently resides in Oakville, Ontario. Joyce's early years were spent training and dancing with the Royal Winnipeg Ballet. She credits her childhood love of bright colours as the foundation of her artistic style. All her fabrics are specially prepared to retain original texture, colour and beauty. Recent juried shows include The Common Thread (1998), the Heart of London Show and Sale (1999) and Le Chassy D'or - France (2000).

Deanne Fitzpatrick works as an artist creating one-of-a-kind hand hooked rugs from recycled wool cloth. Her pieces are inspired by her childhood in Newfoundland, as well as life around her in Cumberland County, Nova Scotia. Her art has been acquired as part of the permanent collections of The Canadian Museum of Civilization, The Art Gallery of Nova Scotia, The Art Gallery of Newfoundland and Labrador, and the Nova Scotia Art Bank.

Myrna Harris A graduate of the Saskatoon City Hospital School of Nursing, Harris began to develop her artistic skills by experimenting with and taking classes in painting, drawing, and pottery. Turning for a time to weaving, she was won over by the technique of felting. Her landscapes portray the land outside her studio and in her memory with dyes and wools, paints and appliqués. She has had several solo and group exhibitions and continues to explore the possibilities of felt.

Margi Hennen has been celebrating the feminine form in funny fabric dolls since 1987, when she graduated from the Nova Scotia College of Art and Design. She is currently living in Winnipeg. "Like Dame Edith Evans, I seem to have a lot of people inside me. My work is about women, humour, and fabric - three of my favourite things."

William Hodge is an honour graduate of the Ontario College of Art, where he has taught since 1967. His work spans all areas of the fibre arts. As a partner in Armure Studios, he produces large-scale architectural tapestries, fine hand-woven fabrics for garments and interiors as well as work involving beading techniques, handmade paper, and stitchery. Hodge has exhibited his work across North America and is represented in corporate and public collections in Canada, the United States and Japan.

Jean Kares Born and educated in the United States, Kares now lives in Vancouver, British Columbia and currently acts as an advisor to CARFAC BC and the Textile Arts Program at Capilano College. She has been involved in Canada's art and craft community for over 20 years and has exhibited her work nationally and in the US in juried, curated, and solo shows. In addition to maintaining a working studio/gallery and exhibiting her work, Kares shares her insights and experience through teaching others about textile processes and creative inspiration.

Jane Kidd was born in Victoria, British Columbia and completed her formal art training at the Vancouver School of Art and the University of Victoria. She is currently teaching at the Alberta College of Art and Design. She works primarily in the textile medium of woven tapestry, which she finds best allows her to express experiences and indulge her inclination towards intricate detail, rich colour, and sensuous surfaces.

Beverley McInnes, a multi-media fibre embroiderer who makes bags and purses, was born in Montreal and now lives in Chester, Nova Scotia. As a juried Master Artisan of The Nova Scotia Designer Crafts Council, she has taught and studied throughout North America and the United Kingdom. She manipulates beads and applies found objects to capture the "look" or image in her mind. McInnes exhibits widely while designing and stitching her unique commissioned purses, neck pouches, and mounted stitcheries.

Alma Newton was born in England, and came to Canada over thirty years ago. Newton turns what has been considered 'women's work' - sewing - into a woman's wonder. Recycling remnants of material, she takes what has been discarded and elevates it into magical cameos of life. She obtained a Diploma in Fine Arts with Distinction from the Alberta College of Art and Design in 1995. She earned her Bachelor of Fine Arts in 1999. In addition to creating her unusual art pieces, she also designs and makes costumes for the theatre and was nominated for a Betty Mitchell Award in 1998. She won an inaugural *Life Begins at 60* Award of Accomplishment in Visual Arts in October 1999. Her work graces both public and private collections across Canada and the United States.

Marianne Parsons Over the past 25 years, Marianne Parsons has been using the quilting stitch as a design tool to portray ideas about things that affect her life. Before taking up quilt-making, she was a recognized embroidery and watercolour artist. Friends and her garden are often featured in her paintings and quilts. Her teaching career has included elementary school, adult education, and quilting guilds across Western Canada. Her contemporary fibre pieces have been juried into national and international shows since 1993. She also enjoys writing about quilt-making.

Sybil Rampen With degrees in Fine Arts and Teaching, Rampen has spent many years studying and experimenting with embroidery. She lectures and also teaches experimental embroidery and watercolour print-making at her Joshua Creek Studio and Gallery in Oakville, Ontario.

Sylvia Ridgway is a non-traditional batik artist working out of her home studio in Victoria, Prince Edward Island. Batik is an ancient technique of fabric decoration using a wax resist method. Ridgway is self-taught and the images and colours of Prince Edward Island are captured in her unique landscapes and flowers, evocative of watercolour paintings.

ARTISTS

Marion Spanjerdt was trained in fashion illustration and graphic design in the Netherlands before immigrating to Canada. Her strong interest in textiles and colour led her to producing banners, wallhangings, and embellished clothing in fabric collage and machine embroidery. Workshops have taken her across Canada and the United States to Hawaii, New Zealand, and Australia. She has participated in many exhibitions, and her commissioned work can be seen in buildings in Sudbury, Toronto, Holland, and the Children's Hospital Centre in Boston. Spanjerdt's current work focuses on private commissions and workshops.

Betty Weaver "My cloth is a reflection of human society. The basic structure of weaving is a framework that fixes an order and an inclination to define patterns. My weavings symbolize journeys and adaptations. Designed to be either hung or wrapped around the body, the pieces provide a tactile and visible form for the protective and comforting nature of our heritage, and the threads that link our common experience, our learning, our interdependence."

Angelika Werth began her career in fashion in Europe, where she worked with Yves St. Laurent in Paris and took a degree as a master dressmaker-designer. She moved to Canada in 1974, settled in Vancouver, and turned to quilting in 1985. The initial inspiration for her Brassieres Series was women and breast cancer, but this has since expanded to embrace issues relating to birth, midlife, relationships, society, religion, and love.

Christel Wille is a weaver/designer with 25 years of practical experience and a lifelong appreciation of all textile media. In 1990, she received the Ontario Handweavers and Spinners Master Weavers Certificate with honours. She participates regularly in juried exhibitions, has won many awards, and teaches both privately and publicly. She designs and weaves silk, rayon, and chenille scarves and wraps under the business name *CW Textile Designs* and is the originator of the Oakville Festival for Fibre Arts.

ACKNOWLEDGEMENTS

The publishers gratefully acknowledge permission to reproduce copyright material. Every effort has been made to trace copyright holders, but in a few cases this has proved impossible. The publishers apologize for any errors or omissions and would like to hear from any copyright holders not acknowledged.

Elizabeth Ann Anderson: "Draw up a design..." from *Colour All My Wings: A Poetry Journey*. Norval: Moulin, 1998. **Margaret Atwood**: "...a fistful of gathered..." from *Some Objects of Wood and Stone*. Toronto: House of Anansi, 1966. "This is the solstice..."; "Winter, Time to eat fat..."; "the green wreaths..."; "We will go around..." from *Morning in the Burned House*. Reprinted by permission of McClelland & Stewart, Inc. The Canadian Publishers. **Margaret Avison**: "Women are breadwinners..." from *Not Yet But Still*. Hantsport: Lancelot Press, 1997. **Marie-Claire Blais**: "My children..." from *Veiled Countries Lives*. Trans. Michael Harris. Montreal: Vehicule Press, 1984. **Roo Borson**: "The wind wants..." from *The Whole Night Coming Home*. Toronto: McClelland & Stewart Inc. The Canadian Publishers, 1984. **Linda M. Brissett**: " I hug life gently..." from *Sunshine in the Shadows*. New York: Vantage Press, 1993. **W. Wilfred Campbell**: "That night I felt..." from "How Winter Came in the Lake Region" (1893); "Soft fall the February snows..." from "Beyond the Hills of Dreams" (1899); "Now by the brook..." from "Indian Summer" (1889). **Bliss Carman**: *A Northern Vigil* from Canadian Poetry Volume One; "The lifelong day..." from "The Eavesdropper" (1893). **George Elliott Clarke**: "I step through snow..." *(Blank Sonnet)*; "I quilt, planting..." *(Quilt)*: "snow on green branches..." *(Early Spring)* from *Wylah Falls*. Reprinted by permission of Polestar Book Publishers. **Leonard Cohen**: "During the day..." from *Stranger Music*. Reprinted by permission of McClelland & Stewart, Inc. The Canadian Publishers. **Isabella Valancy Crawford**: "...buy roses, roses, roses" from "The Roman Rose Seller." **Laura Barbara Dixon**: "Church Bells ring joyfully..."; "I opened my eyes..." from *Changing Seasons*, Milton: Laura Barbara Dixon, 1997. **Lenny Everson**: "Then she knew...". All rights reserved by the author. **Ralph Gustafson**: "A little soup..." from *Tracks in the Snow*. Lantzville: Oolichan, 1994. **David Helwig**: "The picnic chairs..."; "Out of the black soil..."; "Today the leaves..." from *Figures in a Landscape*. Ottawa: Oberon Press, 1967. **Rita Joe**: "I believe in fate..." from *Song of Rita Joe: Autobiography of a Mi'kmaq Poet*. Charlottetown: Ragweed Press, 1996. **Pauline Johnson**: "August is laughing..." from "The Song My Paddle Sings" (1895). **A. M. Klein**: "Muffle the wind..." from poem entitled "Of Nothing at All: Orders" from *The Collected Poems of A. M. Klein*. Compiled with introduction by Miriam Waddington, Toronto, New York: McGraw Hill Ryerson, 1974. **Robert Kroetsch**: "life isn't so bad..."; "Inside the pumpkin..." from *The Stone Hammer Poems*. Reprinted by permission of Oolichan Books. **Archibald Lampman**: "The crunching snowshoes..." from "Winter Uplands" (1900); "The hills grow wintery white..." from "In November" (1888). **Dennis Lee**: "There is a joy of being..." from *The Gods*. Reprinted by permission of McClelland & Steward, Inc. The Canadian Publishers. **Dorothy Livesay**: "So, tip toe as a dancer..."; "Then kiss me!..."; "Life for my kid..."; "In her cupboard..."; "the world chuckling sideways..."; "My old face..."; from *Archive for Our Times: Previously Uncollected and Unpublished Poems of Dorothy Livesay*. Vancouver: Arsenal Pulp Press, 1998. **Anne Marriott**: "The wheat was embroidering..." from *The Wind Our Enemy*. Toronto: Ryerson, 1939. **Anne Michaels**: "The best teacher..."; "But sometimes the world..." from *Fugitive Pieces*. Reprinted by permission of McClelland & Stewart, Inc. The Canadian Publishers. **Sparling Mills**: "I see the importance...". All rights reserved by the author. **L. M. Montgomery**: "This day she picked roses..." from "Aunt Olivia's Beau" in the *Chronicles of Avonlea* (1910). **Susanna Moodie**: "as I could not aid in subduing..." from *Roughing it in the Bush* (1852). **G. E. Morgan**: "Poetry, rocks, and husbands..."; "On a solitary rock they stood..."; "There is no chill so deep..." [Unpublished] Reprinted by permission of the author. **bp Nichol**: "We wed words to things..." from *Selected Poems: the arches*. Ed. Frank Davey. Vancouver: Talon Books, 1980. **P. K. Page**: "it is like a treacle..." from *The Hidden Room: Collected Poems (Vol. 2)*. Erin: The Porcupine's Quill, 1997. **Al Purdy**: "A country of quiescence..." from *Rooms for Rent in the Outer Planets*. Reprinted by permission of Harbour Publishing. **Raymond Queneau**: "The mollusk..." from *French Poetry Today: A Bilingual Anthology*. Ed. Simon Watson Taylor. London: Andre Deutsch, 1974. **Charles D. Roberts**: "I am the spirit astir..." from Autochthon (1899). **Joe Rosenblatt**: "Bees are truck drivers..." from *Top Soil*. Erin: Press Porcepic, 1976. **Charles Sangster**: "The silver-sinewed arms..." from "The Thousand Islands: The St. Lawrence and the Saguenay" (1856). **Robert Service**: "Don't you remember..." from *The Spell of the Yukon* (1907). **Carol Shields**: "Work is...the alarm..."; "Happiness grows..."; "She may yearn to know..."; "Work's not just sitting..." from *The Stone Diaries*. Toronto: Random House of Canada, 1993. **Raymond Souster**: "One red cardinal..." from *The Collected Poems of Raymond Souster*. Ottawa: Oberon, 1980. **Catherine Parr Traill**: "There is no season..." from *Lost in the Backwoods*. **Gilles Vigneault**: "My country's not a country..." from song entitled "Mon Pays" (words and music by Gilles Vigneault); can be found on: *Mon Pays* (1966) - Columbia FL - 334/FS-634 [V] or *Chemin Faisant, Cent et une chansons* (1990) - disque 3 - Le Nordet GVNC 1017/Distribution Musicor; used as translated in: Berton, Pierre. *Winter*. Don Mills: Stoddart, 1994. **Miriam Waddington**: "May was a wonderful country..."; "...the forsythia bush..." from *Collected Poems*. Toronto: Oxford University Press, 1986. Reprinted by permission of Oxford University Press. **Phyllis Webb**: "The shape of prayer..." from *Even Your Right Eye*. Toronto: McClelland & Stewart, Inc. The Canadian Publishers. 1956. **Anne Wilkinson**: *Still Life* Gage Educational Publishing Company.